CW01367729

Your Turn

26 weeks to become a competent manager

BERYL CUCKNEY

authorHOUSE®

AuthorHouse™ UK Ltd.
500 Avebury Boulevard
Central Milton Keynes, MK9 2BE
www.authorhouse.co.uk
Phone: 08001974150

© 2009 Beryl Cuckney. All rights reserved.
Front cover photo and illustrations - Carina Eastwood
No part of this book may be reproduced, stored in a retrieval system, or transmitted by any means without the written permission of the author.

First published by AuthorHouse 3/4/2009

ISBN: 978-1-4389-2981-1 (sc)

www.yourturn.me.uk

Printed in the United States of America
Bloomington, Indiana

This book is printed on acid-free paper.

Foreword

It is a long time since I first entered the world of management – as a 19 year old in an inner city social security office. I was very fortunate to have a line manager who took the time to help me take my first steps. When I made mistakes, which happened often and some of which were expensive, she recognised that they were genuine. She helped me understand where I went wrong and I put them right.

Since then I have spent over 20 years managing and leading in different scenarios and companies, both public and private, in the UK and across the world. I have gained experience and lots of stories and developed my own style. I have been privileged to meet literally thousands of managers at different stages of their careers whilst I have designed and run management development programmes.

My observation is that management as a skill that can be learned and applied in everyday life seems to be eroding. Line managers have little time to share their knowledge and skills. People are promoted into responsible positions with little support. They just work harder and harder, hoping to deliver the right results.

It does not have to be like this. The requirements of your job will not slow down to allow you to learn at your own pace. But there are some key lessons that if you learn at the outset of your management career will stay with you throughout it. Your team deserves to have the best manager possible.

That is what has lead me to write you this book of management briefings, that you may not feel overwhelmed by the range of issues you will face immediately you begin to lead a team. If a situation arises with which you are unfamiliar don't feel guilty – look it up or refer it to your manager.

I hope you find that this book takes some of the pressure off and helps you get real fulfilment as you start out in your management career.

An introduction

There are certain times in our lives when we realise we need to learn quickly – however we may not be sure what we have to learn.

Becoming a manager or supervisor is one of these times. From day 1 you are paid to do the work of a manager and carry the accountability for delivering results.

But what is it you have to do? You were probably very good technically at your job before and this will give you some credibility. Now you will find there are parts of your new job which you need to learn.

It may be tempting in the very first week to try and prove you are the best manager there has ever been – many of these people burn out. They shout loudly and are surprised that within a matter of days they are the least liked and least respected member of the team.

Your new line manager may or may not be good at coaching you into your new role. You are actually now expected to take responsibility for your own development. This is why this series of 26 management briefings has been collated, to help you and your manager through the first 26 weeks of your new management role.

The range of subjects you see listed over the page cover the issues you will regularly come across. Each week you will focus on one of them. For each one there are

- two pages of information
- five questions for a half hour discussion with your manager or mentor
- space for your notes
- an action plan.

26 briefings and where you find them

Chapter **Page**

1. Your role as a manager ... 1
2. Keeping legal, healthy and safe ... 7
3. Your management portfolio ... 13
4. Dress and speech ... 19
5. Company values ... 25
6. Problem solving ... 31
7. Money and fraud ... 37
8. Holidays, sickness and other absence ... 43
9. Management techniques ... 49
10. Using your manager ... 55
11. Building relationships ... 61
12. Appraisal and disciplinary action ... 67
13. Statistics and reporting ... 73
14. Feedback and informal reviews ... 79
15. Empowerment and delegation ... 85
16. Objective setting ... 91
17. Planning ... 97
18. Serving customers ... 103
19. Creating personal impact ... 109
20. Team meetings ... 115
21. Getting people to listen ... 121
22. Managing conflict ... 127
23. Motivating and understanding people ... 133
24. Developing colleagues ... 139
25. Using technology ... 145
26. How am I doing? ... 151

Half hour with your manager or mentor

It is very important that you and your manager or mentor set aside regular time to discuss your development at the outset of your new role. It will not only provide you with answers, but help you understand how your manager thinks and makes decisions. You will build respect and trust in one another as you go along.

The questions suggested for each week provide good guidelines, but do raise other relevant questions as necessary. Try and keep the meeting to half an hour, otherwise you will end up with so much information you will not have time to do anything with it.

- Identify with your manager or mentor a time slot in the week when you can book in your meeting
- Agree where the meetings will be

Notes from the week

It is a good management habit to start keeping a notebook or diary of happenings each week. You will need to account for how you spend your time. Much of your work will not be visible to others. It is only when you deliver results that you will have anything to show for your efforts.

These management notes will become a good reference point for you. I would encourage you to pause for half an hour at the end of each week and reflect back on what has happened relevant to that week's subject. We learn a lot through reflection, and if your job role is very demanding through the day, you will need to take time out to think.

You don't have to just write your thoughts – draw as well. Use colour – one of those 4 colour pens is very useful. If you are familiar with mind-mapping use that to collect your thoughts. Doing this regularly will keep your mind fresh, enabling you consistently to make good quality management decisions.

Putting feet to your decisions...

Having thought about what has happened during the week, you then need to take action. No matter how small the action, it will be a step in the right direction. In this book we will call this doing a "FROG".

Each week decide on:

F **first** thing that you need to do or find out

R **resources** - what do you already have in your kit bag to help you do it

O **others** - any help you need from anyone else to make it happen and why you think this

G **go** - a definite step which you can take immediately to put feet to your decision.

Week by week you may not think you are learning much. But when you look back over the 6 months you will find it very useful to reread your thoughts and comments. This is especially true if you are the sort of person who loves to throw themselves into the job and learn by experience. You will be amazed by the progress that you have made in 6 short months.

1 Your role as a manager

Congratulations on your new job

It is always exciting to start a new job, but this one is particularly important. Your performance is now dependent on how you manage people and resources, rather than your own technical brilliance. In this section you will look at what a manager's role is within your business. By the end you will know

- what your company expects of a manager
- what you should aim to achieve in your first 26 weeks
- what type of issues you should refer to your manager
- the names of people you will be managing
- any financial responsibilities.

'Them' not 'us'

This phrase is often used by employees when they recognise that you are acting on behalf of management. This can be difficult for you at the beginning of your management role for two reasons

- your management colleagues do not yet see you as an experienced colleague and you may not naturally be invited into important meetings and discussions
- you relate better to non-management employees.

To get past this phase of your new job establish your credentials. You got the job on merit. Build on this, learn quickly and work hard. Be clear about the results you need to achieve. Get to know your people, let them get to know you.

If you were promoted and are still in the same department you may need to distance yourself from your old colleagues to avoid any type of favouritism. Build up your new networks. Find colleagues in your new peer group. Work confidently, not arrogantly. Expect to learn a lot in the first weeks. This series of management briefings will help you do this in a structured way during your first six months in the job.

Delivering results

You are likely to be joining a team that was functioning well before you came (or that is what you will be told). What matters now is how you deliver results using the resources available to you. You may feel like changing a number of things. If you find there was something that was stopping the team working effectively, do something to change it. Otherwise, if this is your first management position, consider leaving things as they are for the first few weeks. Changing things can have some unwelcome side effects, which you do not need to create just yet. The team will give you a brief honeymoon period to settle in.

At the team leader or supervisor level of management it is all about consistently delivering the right results today. You are not alone. You have management colleagues working in similar teams and you have your own line manager. The first 26 weeks of your job are key to your management career. Many managers still remember the lessons they learnt in these weeks. You may get the opportunity to go on some management training in due course, but a lot of management decisions are commonsense. Most of us manage our lives outside of work, and many of these skills are what you use at work as well.

You may have heard the terms of 'management' and 'leadership'. In your first weeks concentrate on **management** which means 'doing things right'. If you do this, you will quickly build up experience which will help you make bigger and better decisions.

Half hour with your manager

1. What does my company expect from me now that I am a manager?

2. What do I want to have achieved within my first 26 weeks as a manager? (Check with your manager whether this is realistic.)

3. What people am I responsible for?

4. What money am I responsible for? (You may not have an actual financial budget immediately, but find out what costs you are influencing)

5. What type of issues should I refer to your instead of dealing with myself?

Notes from the week

Putting feet to your decisions...

This is your first opportunity to take a FROG decision based on your learning this week. Management is about making decisions and then acting on them, so here's your chance.

F **first** thing that you need to do or find out _____

_____

_____

R **resources** - what do you already have in your kit bag to help you

_____

_____

O **others** - any help you need from anyone else to make it happen and why you think this _____

_____

_____

G **go** - a definite step which you will take immediately to put feet to your decision _____

_____

_____

2 Keeping legal, healthy and safe

Employment law

When an employer offers a contract of employment and it is accepted by the employee, they have entered into a binding agreement which is covered by civil law. There is a promise to pay wages in exchange for a promise to be available for work. You are now managing a part of your business on behalf of the owner and he or she is trusting you to manage within the law.

At its most fundamental, you are responsible for

- the way you speak to your team, treating all as equal, whatever their age, gender, religion, race
- being familiar with company policy, working to it yourself, and requiring your staff to do so
- identifying any job performance irregularities and discussing these with your manager
- fairly recording employee's achievements so that they can be appropriately rewarded.

Your HR (Human Resources or Personnel) team is your first place to go for advice. They will be able to access expert help if it is required. You must operate within company policy. Even when you do, staff can still take a company to court, challenging company policy. You will read in the news about people who have taken their employers to court for unfair or constructive dismissal, or for discrimination at work.

How do I work within the law?

Treat people as people. Focus on developing the skills they need for the job. Talk regularly with everyone, and make sure everyone has the opportunity to work to their greatest potential. If ever you are in any doubt refer to your line manager.

Health and safety (H&S)

The law places a duty on everyone to behave in a way that is unlikely to cause harm to others. It imposes a duty on employers to take reasonable care of their employees during the course of their employment. H&S is about preventing accidents. If there is an accident at work it must be entered in the accident book.

Your responsibility covers those who work in an office, on customer sites, at home and whilst travelling on official business. Some of the ways that companies manage H&S are by having

- risk assessments for all areas where your employees work
- correct equipment and clothing available
- correct training in use of equipment.

Some ways you can become more H&S conscious

- check all employees have the tools to do the job
- check for trip hazards and trailing wires
- make sure employees wear the correct work clothing, including ear plugs, goggles and other safety features
- arrange eyesight tests for those using computers regularly
- repetitive strain injury leads to significant absenteeism – reduce its likelihood
- establish a normal pattern of working hours for employees so that if a person fails to come to work or get home you can check on their safety
- if anyone works alone with high risk customers or walks through built up areas alone, give them a personal alarm.

Half hour with your manager

1. Who is the best person for me to see for an overview on how to avoid discriminatory practices at work?

2. Ask to see any employment policies your company has. These may be in an employee handbook. What decisions will need your signature rather than mine being sufficient?

3. When will I attend an Equal Opportunities or Employment Law seminar?

4. Who is responsible for managing Health and Safety in the company? Who are the First Aid Officers? Where is the accident book?

5. Familiarise myself with the risk assessments for the areas my teams work in.

Notes from the week

Putting feet to your decisions...

This is your first opportunity to take a FROG decision based on your learning this week. Management is about making decisions and then acting on them, so here's your chance.

F **first** thing that you need to do or find out _____

_____

_____

R **resources** - what do you already have in your kit bag to help you

_____

_____

O **others** - any help you need from anyone else to make it happen and why you think this _____

_____

_____

G **go** - a definite step which you will take immediately to put feet to your decision _____

_____

_____

3 Your management portfolio

One of the exciting things about your management job is that you now get to make decisions that affect the health and well-being of your company and employees. You have responsibility for

- money
- people
- customers
- equipment
- processes

Money

Businesses prosper if they have more cash coming in than going out. Cash comes into the business through sales and goes out by spending money on what makes your business work.

If you are in sales make sure your sales team hits target and if possible over-achieves. Ensure sales orders and contracts are watertight so that customers can be invoiced correctly and quickly.

If you manage a delivery team, operate the team efficiently keeping to any cost budgets, quality standards and timescales you are given.

People

You are allocated a certain number of people to work in your team. You will decide how to get the team to work, how to motivate them and how to help them with any problems so that you all meet the targets. You and your team may need to work closely with other teams to make sure all targets are met and jobs are done.

In some businesses the work you are managing will be repetitive and your targets will be very clear. In other businesses you will need to respond flexibly to the various customer orders that are sold.

Customers

Customers are the reason that businesses prosper. It is often quoted that it can cost up to 10 times as much to get a new customer as it does to keep an existing one. This means that you must pay attention to the experience of the customer. If it is excellent, they will come back and may also recommend you to others. If it is bad, they will complain and tell others not to do business with you.

You need to make sure that all in your team know how to serve the customer well. If you do get a complaint, deal with it quickly and efficiently.

Equipment

In order to deliver your company's goods and services to customers, it has bought equipment. This may be computers, machinery, desks, office buildings or transport. The equipment needs to be used to its maximum and cared for well so that the company gets good value for money. (Remember the health and safety points you read in the last chapter.)

Processes

Over the years managers in your company have designed and built a way of working to get the business results. These processes may cover financial record keeping, people management, quality and time, sales invoicing and delivery notices.

Some of these processes are written down, but a lot are passed on by word of mouth. You need to find out the official processes that exist to cover your area of work. Get familiar with them and make sure your team operate them. As you become more experienced you will suggest changes to processes which will help your achieve targets more efficiently.

Half hour with your manager

1. How do my sales or cost targets contribute to the company's results?

2. What other managers and teams do I need to work closely with? How do I get introduced to them, and build up an effective working relationship?

3. If I get a customer complaint, or notice something that might lead to a complaint, what do I do?

4. What equipment am I personally responsible for? If equipment fails, what can I do to get my team back working as soon as possible?

5. What processes and quality standards exist for my area of work? Where do I find them?

Notes from the week

Putting feet to your decisions...

This is your first opportunity to take a FROG decision based on your learning this week. Management is about making decisions and then acting on them, so here's your chance.

F **first** thing that you need to do or find out _____

_____

_____

R **resources** - what do you already have in your kit bag to help you

_____

_____

O **others** - any help you need from anyone else to make it happen and why you think this _____

_____

_____

G **go** - a definite step which you will take immediately to put feet to your decision _____

_____

_____

4 Dress and speech

The way managers dress and speak within the business is watched by all employees. They also notice and comment on how we behave outside the business – what we do in our own time and how we conduct our home lives.

Dress

You may have dress rules in your business due to the type of work you do – uniforms and other work clothing for serving customers or working with machinery. It is essential in these instances that, at all times, you wear the correct uniform and any health and safety features accurately, including eye goggles, ear plugs and safety shoes.

Uniforms are in place to create the right environment to do business. Encourage your employees to adhere to the spirit of the code.

If your business does not have a uniform, it is likely it will have an informal dress code, possibly written into the employee handbook.

At all times make sure you

- look smart enough for people to wish to do business with you
- keep your shoes polished and your finger nails clean
- ensure your hair is clean and tidy
- do not have body odour.

You will be working closely with a lot of different people in a day – customers, managers, contractors, colleagues, employees - you need to maintain a good impression with all of them. Dress is one way in which we develop good first impressions and make people want to do business with us.

Speech

Speaking is one important way we can express our opinions, pass on information and get reactions from others. Employees rely on hearing information and directions from you in order to get on and do their jobs well.

The way we choose to speak and the words we choose to use all make a difference to the messages we are give to those around us. People hear us even when we do not think they are. Many managers are a little shy of speaking out in front of people. This is however a key part of your role, be it in one to one situations or in team meetings.

You can make things easier by doing a little planning

- prepare what you are going to say beforehand
- keep it simple
- only give between 3 and 5 pieces of information at one time
- check that you have understood correctly any information given by your manager
- include the most important points at the beginning of your comments, and repeat them at the end.

There are a few things you can do to make yourself more understandable to others

- speak slowly
- pause at the end of a sentence
- use words that your employees will understand
- give time for people to ask you questions
- in your answers, repeat what you said to begin with, to emphasise the key messages.

Half hour with your manager

1. How should I dress for everyday work, meetings and customer visits?

2. What changes should I make to the way I speak?

3. How do I need my team to look and sound?

4. What are the important messages coming into the business at the moment?

5. What are the most important changes I must make in the way I behave in the business?

Notes from the week

Putting feet to your decisions...

This is your first opportunity to take a FROG decision based on your learning this week. Management is about making decisions and then acting on them, so here's your chance.

F **first** thing that you need to do or find out _____

_____

_____

R **resources** - what do you already have in your kit bag to help you

_____

_____

O **others** - any help you need from anyone else to make it happen and why you think this _____

_____

_____

G **go** - a definite step which you will take immediately to put feet to your decision _____

_____

_____

5 Company values

If we value something it means it matters to us. This is exactly the same with company values. For a number of reasons the values matter to the company and they matter to the customer. As a manager you must make it your business to understand

- why your company values certain behaviours above others, and
- what you must do to make sure you and your team demonstrate them in the way you work.

Where values come from

As a company grows it develops ways of working which attract customers to spend money. Very often these values are ones which the original owner of the business had. If you work in a large company, look up its history on the website. You will often see that the founders of the company had a vision of serving a certain community or producing a product which would have a specific end result. If you are in a smaller company it is less likely to be written down and you will need to ask the company owner what he or she is aiming to achieve with their business.

Examples of values

In most larger companies these behaviours or values are clearly defined. They reflect the type of environment which will attract customers and employees to the company and will deliver the service that the customer is paying for. Some examples are

- enthusiasm
- integrity
- passion for service
- can-do attitude
- self-awareness
- accuracy
- humility
- simplicity

How values are seen and measured

Senior management must make clear how they want to do business, so that managers like you can carry out your work in the right way. Company values are normally built into

- performance management and appraisal systems - you may already be familiar with them from appraisals you have had in the past. Now you start observing how your team operates so you are able to give them feedback
- training and development – in-house training offered by your company will help you learn the values
- decisions in management meetings
- marketing materials - posters or small leaflets around the office or for customers and on the website.

Have a look at your company website and look up the values of your competitors as well. This will show you how customers can make a choice not only on the products you are selling but also how you do business with them.

Observe how your colleagues interact with one another and customers on the phone, by email, in writing, how they build quality into a product they are working on, how they deal with complaints and work with 3rd parties and contractors.

As you are managing front line colleagues it is very important that you make sure the company values are represented in every aspect of their work. They will translate into different activities depending on the type of front line work you are managing.

Half hour with your manager

1. What are the values of this business and why?

2. Which ones are the most important to my area of work and how might we demonstrate them?

3. What must I do as a manager to show the values?

4. What do I do if a colleague does not behave according to the values?

5. How is my management performance measured against the values?

Notes from the week

Putting feet to your decisions...

This is your first opportunity to take a FROG decision based on your learning this week. Management is about making decisions and then acting on them, so here's your chance.

F **first** thing that you need to do or find out _____

_____

_____

R **resources** - what do you already have in your kit bag to help you

_____

_____

O **others** - any help you need from anyone else to make it happen and why you think this _____

_____

_____

G **go** - a definite step which you will take immediately to put feet to your decision _____

_____

_____

6 Problem solving

A problem occurs when something happens which you and others cannot solve immediately. When you first start as a manager you may think that everything is a problem and you constantly have to ask someone for help.

Don't worry – you will soon get to know a lot more of your company's procedures. It is often better to ask someone rather than make up a solution which is wrong. No manager knows the answer to everything. It is the way you deal with problems and how you manage any consequences of your decisions that is important.

For now we will sort problems into two types

- expected
- unexpected

Expected problems

There are certain problems which arise in the normal course of your work. They may be to do with

- quality of materials
- machine failure
- customer complaints
- clash of holiday requests
- poor work performance or sickness.

You need to implement the solutions that your company expects. Procedures are written down which will answer many of these problems for you. Glance through the contents page of guidance manuals on your manager's bookshelf to get an idea of what is covered. Your intranet site will give you guidance. There will be experts in the business who can also give you help, for example Health and Safety and Personnel or HR.

Unexpected problems

An unexpected problem is one that has not been planned for by your company. There are no answers in any of the books. When considering how to solve such a problem the first step is to get good information. This information should tell you

- what needs to happen as a result of your decision
- the impact you do or do not want your decision to have on people
- the time available to you in people-hours to solve the problem and to carry out your decision
- the money you may need to spend or save.

From this information you need to try and deduce the true facts. This is where you need to use your wisdom. There is no such thing as a difficult person, just a difficult situation. Identifying the true facts is the first step towards taking any personal feeling out of the situation. Personal feeling will not generally lead you to a good decision.

When you are sure you have the right facts, check to see if company policy and procedures exist to solve the problem. Sometimes your instinct may lead you to solve a problem in a certain way. More normally at this early stage in your management career you need to use the experience of those around you.

When to use your manager

If the problem continues is it likely to have catastrophic consequences in the very near future for personal safety or the company's good? If so, go straight to your line manager and speak it through. If the consequences are likely to be serious but not immediate, bring it up with your manager at the earliest opportunity.

Half hour with your manager

1. List five problems that arise during the week

2. Which ones are likely to happen again? Plan to avoid them.

3. Which ones were not avoidable and may happen again?

4. Ask two of my new management colleagues about problems they remember facing when they first started – what did they do?

5. What room for error is there in my team's work? How can I let people learn from mistakes?

Notes from the week

Putting feet to your decisions...

This is your first opportunity to take a **FROG** decision based on your learning this week. Management is about making decisions and then acting on them, so here's your chance.

F **first** thing that you need to do or find out _____

_____

_____

R **resources** - what do you already have in your kit bag to help you

_____

_____

O **others** - any help you need from anyone else to make it happen and why you think this _____

_____

_____

G **go** - a definite step which you will take immediately to put feet to your decision _____

_____

_____

7 Money and fraud

Successful businesses exist because

- they maintain a flow of cash, which means they can pay their bills
- they make a profit, which can either be paid to employees in bonuses or invested for future growth.

Managers are entrusted with keeping the company financially healthy. Money is created or spent in a number of ways

- income from sales
- costs of sale
- general expenses of running business
- losses or scrap (wasted resource)
- time of employees
- customers retained

What you can do to make the money go further

You will probably find that you have targets which you and your team need to meet. By meeting these targets you are doing your bit to help the company keep financially healthy. As you begin your job make sure you at least meet these targets.

As you gain more experience you may find your manager asks you to review the way you and your team work so that you can achieve higher targets. This may include

- higher productivity per hour or day
- buying more items out of the same budget
- getting more things right first time
- less time on each customer transaction
- speeding up a process
- reducing or getting rid of overtime.

Team members often have ideas of how to save money – make time to listen carefully to them.

Fraud

Fraud is stealing. It is the easiest way for someone to end their career. The first point here is that you must never respond to the temptation to be involved in corporate fraud. If someone asks you to be part of it, speak with your line manager immediately.

How people defraud a company

Typical ways in which someone defrauds a company are

- giving confidential company information to a competitor
- using company information for personal benefit
- taking equipment like stationery or components
- wasting company time which they are paid for
- absenting themselves from work for no acceptable reason.

Why people commit fraud

It can be for many reasons but two main reasons are

Financial
If you know or hear that someone in your team is in trouble financially, mention it to your manager. They will be able to have a conversation with them and if their work involves them dealing with money, can determine whether they need to be moved to another job where money is not a temptation.

Grudge against the company
A person may believe they are being treated unfairly by the company and fraudulent activity is their way of retaliation. You are more likely to find this out by having good working relationships with all your team. Then you will spot odd behaviour.

Half hour with your manager

1. How am I and my team spending or saving the company money?

2. How do my targets impact on the company's financial performance?

3. Where am I wasting money?

4. How are ideas mentioned by the team considered?

5. What do I do if I think someone is defrauding the company? Give me some examples where it has happened.

Notes from the week

Putting feet to your decisions...

This is your first opportunity to take a FROG decision based on your learning this week. Management is about making decisions and then acting on them, so here's your chance.

F **first** thing that you need to do or find out _____

_____

_____

R **resources** - what do you already have in your kit bag to help you

_____

_____

O **others** - any help you need from anyone else to make it happen and why you think this _____

_____

_____

G **go** - a definite step which you will take immediately to put feet to your decision _____

_____

_____

8 Holidays, sickness and other absence

When a person signs a contract of employment they are saying that they will

- report for work for a certain number of hours each day or week
- keep themselves fit and healthy for work.

This means that employees have a duty to come to work unless their absence is pre-authorised or they are sick.

Holidays

Most employers recognise that an employee will work better if they have some relaxation during the year. A holiday entitlement every 12 months is usually written into their contract. When someone has a part-time or job-sharing contract their holiday entitlement is often calculated in hours, not days. Holiday entitlement may increase over the course of employment due to length of service or promotion. Individuals are notified of this by management.

Although the employee has the right to these holidays, they are taken at the discretion of management, to fit in with work requirements. This is why holiday scheduling can be complex at school holiday times when a greater number of people may want the same time off work. You need to find out

- how much holiday everyone is entitled to
- when the leave year starts and ends
- how the scheduling has been decided up till now.

A word of warning – your colleagues will be used to how the holidays are allocated. Don't change the system unless it is clearly unfair. If it does need to change, wait until you have been in your job a good few months.

No employee has a right to national holidays (bank holidays). Many employers will add them to the holiday entitlement, with people taking them on the appropriate day. Companies that work globally or who do shift work may decide to use the bank holiday system in a different way. You need to check what happens in your company.

Paid holidays are for relaxation, they are not for people to do other paid work. If you notice that a person is using their holiday to work for someone else, raise it with your manager.

Sickness

At all times you want the workplace to be an environment where employees can work to the best of their abilities. Many companies have guidelines as to what to do if an employee does call in sick. If a person is unfit to work they must contact their manager at the earliest opportunity. You will need to know the nature of their illness and how long they are likely to be away. Employees can generally self-certify their sickness for the first few days off. Thereafter they must get a doctor's note.

If a person does not turn up to work they must be contacted. It may be they have been in an accident on the way to work, and you are the first person to notice their absence.

Other absence

Employees may need extra time off work – on compassionate grounds. This could be for a family bereavement or because a family member is unexpectedly ill and needs short-term care. These absences may be authorised as paid or unpaid time off. These decisions will be taken by your manager or Personnel/HR.

Half hour with your manager

1. What holiday entitlement do my employees have?

2. Who manages holiday entitlement?

3. What should happen if someone is off work, sick?

4. What arrangements do I have in place to cover employee absence, short term or long term?

5. What is the process for giving someone time off for reasons other than holiday or sickness?

Notes from the week

Putting feet to your decisions...

This is your first opportunity to take a FROG decision based on your learning this week. Management is about making decisions and then acting on them, so here's your chance.

F **first** thing that you need to do or find out _____
_____
_____

R **resources** - what do you already have in your kit bag to help you
_____
_____

O **others** - any help you need from anyone else to make it happen and why you think this _____
_____
_____

G **go** - a definite step which you will take immediately to put feet to your decision _____
_____
_____

9 Management techniques

Management is a job that is never finished and you are always learning how to do things better. Hour after hour, day after day you are making decisions - some small, some big - but all of which will determine how efficiently you and your team work. Aim to be consistently good at your job and that consistency will mean you become an excellent manager.

What do I spend my time doing?

Your job is a combination of

- planning
- monitoring
- communicating
- motivating.

Planning

When you plan your daily, weekly and monthly work, calculate what your team must achieve, put it into figures if you can, work out what problems might get in your way and how likely they are to happen.

Managers generally plan to over-achieve targets as something always happens which you did not expect. As you grow in experience you will begin to plan more accurately - but to begin with there will be an element of guesswork.

When looking at what work you will do, focus on the areas where your team may need help in order to achieve target, for example, the work is complex or a person is new to the job. Always leave some of your time free so you can respond to emergencies as they arise.

Monitoring

All the work of your team will reflect back on you - not only **what** is done but **how** it is done. When a person knows their work will be checked, they generally pay more attention to it.

Managers usually check a percentage of work and if it is correct you make an assumption that the rest is correct. However, if you find a number of errors, you can choose to check that type of work or that person's work more closely. If your team are interacting directly with the customer, listen-in to their phone calls and look at letters to customers. Remember that emails usually go out without any checks. You may be 'cc'd' on them but it is too late if there is an error.

Communicating

Your team and other managers will expect you to be open and honest in the way you run your work and produce results. You need to give each individual about half an hour of your time once a month when you can informally discuss how the work is going and for them to ask you questions. In this way you can often pre-empt problems.

Many managers have a weekly team briefing where they can officially pass on company information and other news. Book these into the diary so that they happen.

Motivating

You are generally chosen to be a manager as you can be relied on to get good work out of people. Encourage your team to help you find better ways of working. If productivity is too low, find out why people are lacking energy and focus. If people are regularly absent from work, what is putting them off?

Give your team the exciting challenges rather than keeping them for yourself. This will help them develop new skills. Aim to create an atmosphere where people want to work to their highest potential.

Half hour with your manager

1. How do I know the management behaviours and competencies that are expected of me?

2. How often should I have one to one conversations and team briefings?

3. From your experience, does any person in my team need a particular management approach?

4. Can you give me some examples from your experience where you noticed something abnormal, questioned it and uncovered something that was going wrong?

5. What work must I check regularly?

Notes from the week

Putting feet to your decisions...

This is your first opportunity to take a FROG decision based on your learning this week. Management is about making decisions and then acting on them, so here's your chance.

F **first** thing that you need to do or find out _____
_____
_____

R **resources** - what do you already have in your kit bag to help you
_____
_____

O **others** - any help you need from anyone else to make it happen and why you think this _____
_____
_____

G **go** - a definite step which you will take immediately to put feet to your decision _____
_____
_____

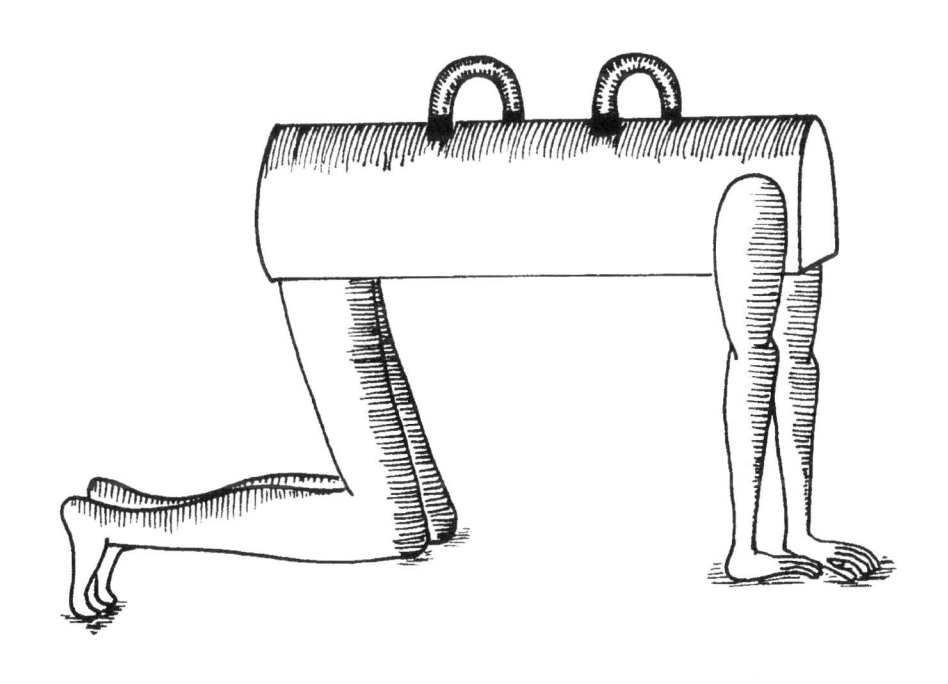

10 Using your manager

The person who most likely wants you to succeed in your management job is your own manager. The better you do, the easier their job is. During these first weeks of your new job you will be taking up quite a bit of their time, so perhaps now is the time for you to take an interest in them and discover the valuable resource you have in them.

Information

Your manager's role is broader than yours. He or she will have ready access to information about the company that you do not have. You need to find out how and when your manager shares information from management meetings and other changes which they hear about. When you are making decisions and your manager gives you advice, don't think they are correcting you. Often their advice will be based on information that you do not know about, or did not realise its importance in the company at the moment.

When you get information from your manager be clear as to whether it is "in confidence" or can be shared with your team. It is important that your manager learns to trust you with information, as the greater the trust the more they will be able to share with you.

Experience

At this early point in your management career you need to learn as fast as possible. One of the best people to learn from is your manager. Most of us like to talk about ourselves and how we have got to where we are. Key moments in our careers remain fresh if we get the chance to talk about them. Use informal moments to ask your manager about

- challenges they have faced and how they dealt with them
- what they enjoy about managing and leading
- how they have progressed in their own career
- their professional background.

Friend and networker

You will be needing friends and others who can open doors for you and with whom you can have light-hearted moments about work situations without fear of it being misinterpreted. One of the most important relationships to build is with your own manager. You don't need to be really pally – this can make it harder to deal with disagreements between you – but you do need to find a way to work together in a relaxed way.

Sounding board

There will be times when you need to talk over situations, not for answers, but to get clarity in your own mind, for example

- a decision you are not sure about
- how to manage conflict between team members
- how to change behaviours.

You may have someone in your team whom you really trust, but who will not understand all the issues you have to consider, and many of these issues will be confidential anyway. It is a good idea if you can use your manager as a sounding board. He or she will usually enjoy having a short meeting with you to talk the problem through. This will clarify things for you both. It also helps them feel more experienced, and mentoring is a key part of their role.

Half hour with your manager

1. What technical knowledge do you have that might be useful to me?

2. What key management lessons have you learned?

3. How often will we have meetings and how can I best prepare myself for them?

4. How is your job different to yours?

5. How do I get the best from you?

Notes from the week

Putting feet to your decisions...

This is your first opportunity to take a FROG decision based on your learning this week. Management is about making decisions and then acting on them, so here's your chance.

F **first** thing that you need to do or find out _____
_____
_____

R **resources** - what do you already have in your kit bag to help you
_____
_____

O **others** - any help you need from anyone else to make it happen and why you think this _____
_____
_____

G **go** - a definite step which you will take immediately to put feet to your decision _____
_____
_____

11 Building relationships

Relationships are vital to business. People choose to work with people they like, whether they are employees or customers. Contracts can be lost because customers lose confidence in an individual with whom they are working. As a manager you are now the official face of your business to your customer.

When relationships will matter

A good working relationship pays dividends at certain times, but particularly

- when you need to get information quickly
- when winning a repeat contract quickly so reducing costs of sale
- when asking a customer to accept a delay in delivery
- at performance appraisal
- when you need to follow disciplinary procedures
- at a busy work time where you need people to put in extra hours or effort.

How to build relationships

Use every opportunity, be it meetings, corridor conversations or joint working to try and build towards mutual respect and trust. You can start the process by three steps

1. make contact with the other person, explaining why you think you it a good idea to get to know one another better
2. take time to understand what they do, and explain your responsibilities clearly
3. accept the other person for what they are - you don't have to agree with everything they say.

Relationships with customers

A customer is anyone who, from time to time, relies on you to deliver a service or product.

If you are in production, working in customer service or sales, your customers are paying customers If you are managing an IT department, work in Personnel or Finance, your customers are your colleagues.

Customers come from diverse backgrounds and cultures. You will need to learn any special etiquette in greeting and speaking with customers whose cultural background is different from yours. Many companies have policies on whether to give or accept gifts. You will need to find out what the policy is in your company and also with your customers.

New relationships with colleagues

Time is precious so you need to choose carefully who you spend time with and why. You may need to review the contacts you have with people with whom you were friendly before your promotion.

Build relationships with

- all your immediate team - each has a personality, range of skills and opinions to offer to the work
- your own manager – in most cases this is possible. Try and ignore other people's opinions of your line manager and create your own impression; it will then be based on truth rather than hearsay
- other managers at your level across the business - together you form a team which is delivering results day after day.

Half hour with your manager

1. Find out how I can build a better relationship with any paying customers.

2. What is thought about my team by the rest of the organisation?

3. What business etiquette do I need to learn to manage relationships with different cultures?

4. What close working relationships did I have before I was promoted which would be better it they ended or changed?

5. What is my company's policy on giving and receiving gifts?

Notes from the week

Putting feet to your decisions...

This is your first opportunity to take a FROG decision based on your learning this week. Management is about making decisions and then acting on them, so here's your chance.

F **first** thing that you need to do or find out _____
_____
_____

R **resources** - what do you already have in your kit bag to help you
_____
_____

O **others** - any help you need from anyone else to make it happen and why you think this _____
_____
_____

G **go** - a definite step which you will take immediately to put feet to your decision _____
_____
_____

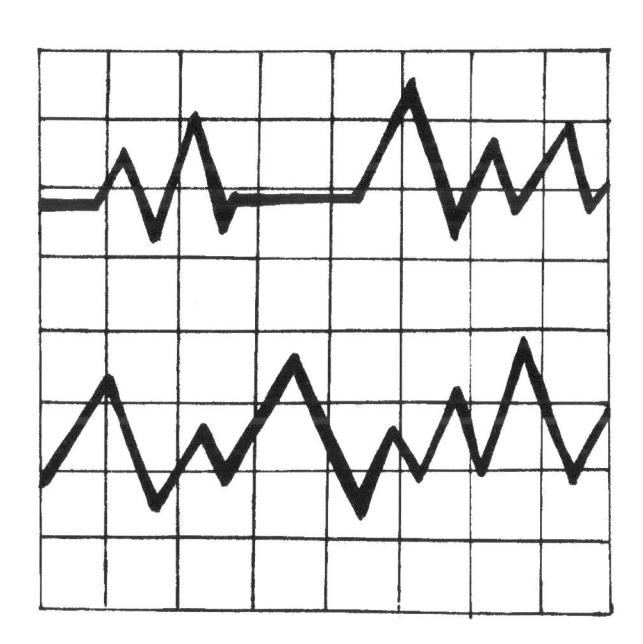

12 Appraisal and disciplinary action

Appraisal is the part of the performance management cycle where you record and discuss responsibilities and achievements. Performance management covers

- objective setting with your manager and planning
- objective setting with your team
- informal and formal reviews
- appraisal.

What appraisal achieves

As with any process, it is only a process; it is **how** you use it that brings the results. If it works well, it can

- motivate employees by giving them work they want to do
- encourage two way communication
- identify existing skills and potential in individuals
- share ideas and solve problems which will improve the business.

What it cannot do is

- put everything right that is wrong in the company enable people to find business that doesn't exist
- turn an unsuitable, perhaps an incompetent person, into a major achiever
- solve personality clashes.

The manager's role

Your role is to

- create an atmosphere in team briefings where it is normal to discuss work
- let everyone know what the business plans to do and work out how they can contribute

- decide if a person needs any training
- give honest feedback during the year
- fairly appraise individual performance.

Why people may not wish to be appraised

People object to appraisal for many reasons. Some say it consumes a lot of time and is non-productive. Appraisal meetings may be badly handled and the line manager seen as incompetent especially if you have had personality clashes which may prevent objectivity. Some people see written assessment as a threat.

Disciplinary action

Employees contract with their employer to work to the best of their abilities and deliver the required work. It is important for you to learn that the effectiveness of the business can be undermined if issues relating to capability and performance are not handled professionally and consistently, or, even worse, if such matters are ignored altogether.

There will be procedures in your company as to how to deal with these situations. In the first instance refer any such cases to your line manager who will advise you.

Managing performance fairly

To manage performance fairly requires you to develop good management habits – many of them are those you are learning in these briefings, but

- make sure that you give feedback when you need to and for a good reason.
- apply company procedures correctly and be consistent across the team. By doing this you will stay within employment legislation and you will have created fair and balanced evidence.

This approach will also support any process to dismiss someone on the grounds of unacceptable performance.

Half hour with your manager

1. What is the performance management system used in this company?

2. What training will be available to me on this subject?

3. Is pay or bonus linked to performance? If so, how does this work?

4. Where do I find the guidance on disciplinary matters?

5. In my first year how will I be supported by you whilst managing the performance of my team?

Notes from the week

Putting feet to your decisions...

This is your first opportunity to take a FROG decision based on your learning this week. Management is about making decisions and then acting on them, so here's your chance.

F **first** thing that you need to do or find out _____

_____

_____

R **resources** - what do you already have in your kit bag to help you

_____

_____

O **others** - any help you need from anyone else to make it happen and why you think this _____

_____

_____

G **go** - a definite step which you will take immediately to put feet to your decision _____

_____

_____

13 Statistics and reporting

Managing and reporting information is crucial to achieving targets. It includes

- storing information so you can retrieve it
- working with data protection legislation
- exchanging information with colleagues
- making decisions based on accurate data.

It is really important that you report the true figures. Anything else will lead to wrong conclusions. Do not cover up a poor performance or exaggerate good figures. Once you start on this road it is very difficult, if not impossible, to start telling the truth again.

Information that must be reported

You manager will tell you the information you must report as it will contribute to their management reporting. It may include

- sales figures
- quality achieved
- staff absenteeism
- productivity ratios
- budget spend
- number of customers spoken to
- number of complaints

Where do you keep information?

Information can be kept on company computer systems which are specifically designed for it, or in paper records. Information which you write down about individuals' performance must be available to them to read.

Be careful about creating new personal records on the computer as legislation is clear about how long such information can be kept and what security measures should be in place to protect personal details. At the start of your management career you should not need to start keeping new records unless your manager asks you to.

What is done with statistics and reports?

Statistics and reporting information have two key functions

- they tell you how you measure up to targets week by week so if necessary you can make adjustments to the way you and your team are working
- over time you can look at average performance. If you use Excel or a similar IT package you can build graphs which help you analyse variances in performance.

As you get more experienced you may need to put a business case together to get more staff or money or equipment. Often the statistics and reporting you do on a weekly basis will provide you with good quality information on which you can base a request to your manager for more resource.

Once you have reported the true details you then go on to explain why the figures are as they are – this is accountability. This is the time for you to exercise your judgment and opinion.

What is my role in reporting?

- find out what figures you need to report and when
- become familiar with any computer systems or paper records you will complete
- make sure you understand why you are reporting
- translate statistics in a way your team can understand
- start looking at patterns in your reporting which may lead you to manage your team and work differently
- take accurate data to management meetings to help make decisions.

Half hour with your manager

1. What regular figures must I deliver and when?

2. What reporting mechanisms do we have, on-line or on paper?

3. Why are these particular targets important to the company?

4. How can I make the targets motivational and understandable to my team?

5. What things should I be aware of which could affect us hitting target?

Notes from the week

Putting feet to your decisions...

This is your first opportunity to take a FROG decision based on your learning this week. Management is about making decisions and then acting on them, so here's your chance.

F **first** thing that you need to do or find out _____

_____

_____

R **resources** - what do you already have in your kit bag to help you

_____

_____

O **others** - any help you need from anyone else to make it happen and why you think this _____

_____

_____

G **go** - a definite step which you will take immediately to put feet to your decision _____

_____

_____

14 Feedback and informal reviews

What you observe and comment on will provide your team members with an idea of what is important to you. Feedback is a skill and requires careful practice. To do it you need to

- know exactly what you expect to see someone doing in their work
- use factual observations for accuracy
- give feedback regularly and in a way that increases learning and development.

Why is feedback necessary?

Most people come to work wanting to do a great job. Adults generally do not want to keep asking if what they are doing is OK. Hearing from their manager that they are on the right track or that they need to change how they are working, will steadily increase their confidence and help them become a more flexible and useful team member.

Whether or not your performance management system is linked to pay, we should never leave feedback just to the annual formal reviews. Feedback should be a regular part of a conversation between you and your team members. Feedback works both ways. You need to hear how your management style is helping or hindering your team's performance.

Watching your team at work

You need to learn how and what to observe, to help you spot trends of behaviours and results. We observe using the senses – seeing, hearing and feeling. Get used to what you would normally expect to see, hear and feel when your team is delivering good results. You will then much more quickly identify when something changes and be able to give feedback to the whole team or individual.

Rules of giving feedback

Feedback focuses on the value it may have for the receiver, not on the "release" it provides you in giving it. It must always be constructive. It should open up a conversation which will let you discuss the way that a person works. Feedback is most likely to be effective if the person receiving it understands it, accepts it and can build on it. If a person changes their way of working after you have given them feedback, observe it and let them know that their new way is what you were looking for.

When giving feedback you should

- prepare what you need to say
- do it as soon as possible after the event
- say what the behaviour and the effect were
- make it constructive and descriptive
- own the feedback by using 'I' and not 'they'
- ensure the person can change the situation
- ask for mutual ways forward.

What happens after I have given feedback?

It is the responsibility of your team members to decide what to do with your feedback. They have five choices

- they may be aware of the point you raise and want to discuss it with you more
- they may be aware of the point you raise but need time to think before discussing further
- your feedback may be news to them, and they may need more information to understand what you are saying
- your feedback may be news to them and they may want to discuss it immediately
- there may be no need to do anything but thank you for the feedback.

Half hour with your manager

1. How am I getting on so far in my management work? (Make sure your manager describes specific events which you can remember. If they say "You're doing fine" ask why they say that.)

2. What kind of things should I be observing in the workplace, which will tell me that work is progressing normally?

3. Give my manager some feedback on how their management style is helping me.

4. What feedback do you think my team should be hearing that would help them raise or maintain their performance?

5. What are you observing in the way that I am working?

Notes from the week

Putting feet to your decisions...

This is your first opportunity to take a FROG decision based on your learning this week. Management is about making decisions and then acting on them, so here's your chance.

F **first** thing that you need to do or find out _____
_____
_____

R **resources** - what do you already have in your kit bag to help you
_____
_____

O **others** - any help you need from anyone else to make it happen and why you think this _____
_____
_____

G **go** - a definite step which you will take immediately to put feet to your decision _____
_____
_____

15 Empowerment and delegation

Even though you are in charge, do not think that you have to do everything. To begin with you may want to have a tight control over every event. This is not unusual and is probably due to a lack in your own confidence in doing your management duties well. However, to your team you will quickly be accused of micro-managing and they will be telling you to back off. If you can learn to empower your team you will

- give yourself more time to think
- pass on your skills more quickly to others
- be seen as supportive rather than dictatorial.

What are empowerment and delegation?

These words normally mean the same thing. They mean that you are ensuring that decisions are being made at the lowest possible level. This should lead to

- the customer getting the best service
- your team having greater job satisfaction through the responsibility they hold.

In a first line management position you are likely to spend 80% of your time doing hands-on technical work and 20% doing management tasks. You cannot be with your team all the time, so you must decide how to split the work between you and the team.

What cannot be delegated?

It will depend on the type of work you are supervising or managing, but there is very little that cannot be delegated. Performance appraisal and disciplinary matters cannot be delegated. There may also be certain financial and security issues that require your signature.

How do I delegate?

A person needs four things in order to take full responsibility for their results

- information – what they need to know
- resources – to help them do the work
- authority – to make decisions
- accountability – for results, whether good or bad

If these four things are not in place, you are dumping work, not delegating. If you have a performance management system, you would use your objective setting process to agree each person's overall responsibilities. Other opportunities will arise during the normal course of work, for example

- attending a meeting in place of you
- chairing a meeting
- managing a small project
- coaching a new member of staff.

How do I know if I have delegated well?

It depends a bit on the level of competence of each team member but usually you will have a mixture of

- eagerness to be told about new tasks
- hesitancy as to ability to do the task well, but open to advice
- competence
- confidence.

If you are doing too much of the work or have dumped responsibility you may see

- people without enough to do
- boredom
- laziness
- letters of resignation or requests to move teams.

Half hour with your manager

1. What cannot be delegated under any circumstances?

2. Who is my deputy if I am ill or when I am on holiday?

3. How competent and confident are each of the team to have work delegated to them?

4. What parts of my work could I delegate more of?

5. Are there signs of boredom and laziness in the team?

Notes from the week

Putting feet to your decisions...

This is your first opportunity to take a FROG decision based on your learning this week. Management is about making decisions and then acting on them, so here's your chance.

F **first** thing that you need to do or find out _____
_____
_____

R **resources** - what do you already have in your kit bag to help you
_____
_____

O **others** - any help you need from anyone else to make it happen and why you think this _____
_____
_____

G **go** - a definite step which you will take immediately to put feet to your decision _____
_____
_____

16 Objective setting

Managers have to plan to achieve. Objectives help to focus minds on areas which are of direct and vital importance to the business' survival and prosperity, and where the individual can make a difference. Sometimes called key performance indicators, you will agree objectives with the job holder on three occasions

- when they are new to the company or team
- you are at the start of a new appraisal year
- following a mid-term review of performance

How do objectives help me manage?

A responsible manager looks at their team like this

- you are 100% responsible for your team's performance and development
- if they do not perform you have not managed them effectively or you are employing the wrong people
- you are 100% responsible for the quality of communication between your team and you.

Of course, employees have a requirement to deliver their best work, but objective setting gives all of you the opportunity to discuss what work needs doing, how it needs to be done and for the job holders to explain what they would like to achieve from the next year at work.

It is very rewarding once it is right, as

- it frees up much of your time to manage.
- it provides a mechanism for your staff to be motivated to take more responsibility
- you know you have told them the business priorities for the coming year.

Writing objectives

Writing objectives is one of the most difficult and time-consuming management responsibilities. Remember, however difficult you may find it, this is your colleague's future work you are describing so you need to make sure they are interested and the objectives motivational.

A person usually has a maximum of six objectives and a minimum of three. Any more and they will not remember them. Any less and the job is not satisfying. Although you will usually write the objectives, you should agree them with the job holder and be prepared to discuss and change wordings.

The process of setting objectives includes

- agreeing your own objectives with your manager
- deciding how you want to use your team to help you achieve your team goals
- making sure the work reflects the team's level of job responsibility
- deciding what the measures of success will be.

SMART objectives

You'll not be a manager long before you hear SMART. This is a way for you to check the quality of the objectives you write. Each one should be

S pecific	- clear what the action is to be
M easurable	- target is quantifiable
A ttainable	- it is possible to achieve the objective
R ealistic	- more likely than not to be successful
T imebound	- the point when it will be reviewed.

Get it right and your team will be more competent, creative and accountable.

Half hour with your manager

1. When do I get my objectives for the year from you?

2. What is our company's process for writing and recording objectives?

3. Will I get any training on writing objectives?

4. Do you need to see the objectives I write or can I just agree them with the team?

5. From your experience, how do objectives help or hinder me getting the job done?

Notes from the week

Putting feet to your decisions...

This is your first opportunity to take a FROG decision based on your learning this week. Management is about making decisions and then acting on them, so here's your chance.

F   **first** thing that you need to do or find out _____

_____

_____

R   **resources** - what do you already have in your kit bag to help you

_____

_____

O   **others** - any help you need from anyone else to make it happen and why you think this _____

_____

_____

G   **go** - a definite step which you will take immediately to put feet to your decision _____

_____

_____

17 Planning

As a manager other people are relying on you to deliver results consistently. To do this your team and other managers need to know what you need from them in order for you all to be successful. Planning helps you take control and keep control. It also means that if you are away from work, work can continue.

What do I plan?

This will depend on where you work in the company but might include

- scheduling of shifts
- your own time
- work : life balance
- team reviews and personal objectives
- how to achieve daily, weekly, monthly objectives
- who manages which accounts or customers.

Plans always change so why bother?

Many of us are attracted by crisis management. It requires adrenalin. It creates an opportunity for a manager to show leadership. It is fun. But it is also the most expensive way to manage – you have little time to weigh up options efficiently.

Depending on your work requirements plan a week or a month ahead, then you can plan to avoid known crises. You will know what you need to achieve and how it should happen, so if something changes you can flex the plan to suit, or else explain at the earliest opportunity that you may now find it difficult to meet your targets.

The discipline of planning gives you precious time to think. You can incorporate good ideas that your team have shared with you. This shows that you listen to them. You can alternate work duties so that the team develops and does not get bored.

How much time should I use to plan?

At this early stage in your management career it is good to get used to doing it regularly. Give yourself at least one hour each week – the beginning or end of the week is good. Make sure you have a suitable place to sit which is quiet and undisturbed.

An important part of planning is checking that what you planned, happened. If it didn't you should work out why not and what happened instead. You will become an experienced manager more quickly if you do this regularly. Give your brain the chance to make sense of what is going on. By doing this you will find it easier to recall your experiences in the future.

What are the benefits of planning?

You will discover them for yourself, but as a starter

- it is easier for you to be accountable for results
- you can respond confidently to the unexpected
- you develop your team and plan in any training
- a one page plan is a good communication tool
- you can anticipate difficulties creatively
- improve efficiency through identifying repetitive work and finding better ways to do it
- as a manager you are seen to be reliable
- you can find short cuts
- it stops you procrastinating
- you can make time for yourself.

How do I plan?

Keep it simple. Your company may have software to help you plan. If not, draw out a simple table with headings detailing the objective, the resources you need to complete it, the date you will review progress and any remarks. You can share it with your line manager and team who will be able to comment on it and add in their experience and ideas.

Half hour with your manager

1. What parts of my job should I be planning? Are there specific things we have to plan at certain times of the year?

2. What software, if any, should I be using to plan?

3. What things do you know of which might wreck my plans?

4. What planning do you do? Do you share this with me?

5. What is your view of any plans I have done already in my management work?

Notes from the week

Putting feet to your decisions...

This is your first opportunity to take a FROG decision based on your learning this week. Management is about making decisions and then acting on them, so here's your chance.

F **first** thing that you need to do or find out _____

_____

_____

R **resources** - what do you already have in your kit bag to help you

_____

_____

O **others** - any help you need from anyone else to make it happen and why you think this _____

_____

_____

G **go** - a definite step which you will take immediately to put feet to your decision _____

_____

_____

18 Serving customers

Customers are the reason that your company exists. You may have an excellent product or service, you may have a niche in the market – but without enough people buying, you have no business. From a sales perspective it is cheaper and quicker to get more business from an established customer than from a new one. As a first line manager you are key to developing and maintaining healthy relationships with customers and end users.

Why customer service?

Customers make choices. They work with you because you offer a product or service which

- they know they need
- at a price they can afford
- delivered in a way with which they are satisfied.

Sometimes you may find that your company asks you to do things which you know the customer has no interest in. This is inefficient and not value for money. Talk with your manager about these situations.

By talking with a customer, over time you will get to hear all sorts of things about their business; how it is run, their current problems, changes coming up and new products. This is all valuable marketing information for you to pass back into your company.

How do we keep customers?

Some of the things you could focus on are

- thinking of the customer as an individual, not an organisation
- encouraging them to share their views
- inviting feedback on how they see your company
- delivering a good service consistently
- being professional at all times

- keeping them informed of changes in products or in the market place which may affect them
- trying not to deliver surprises.

Getting your team on side

You will often be working or speaking with an end user, not directly with the person who decides whether to spend money with you. End users are like children at the sweet counter – they have no money but are very influential. Each member of your team has a responsibility to help each end user enjoy working with you. This will involve

- reviewing the performance objectives you have set them (by achieving them will they have made a good impression on the customer? Or just on your own company's figures?)
- encouraging them to share information they have about customers at team briefings
- making sure they have the right tools to do the job, even the right clothing, so they are correctly representing your company when with the customer.

Customer Feedback

All feedback is useful. Sometimes we like what we hear, sometimes it is a complaint. Make sure that you respond to all feedback by thanking the customer for taking the time to give it. Feedback is one way a customer has of telling us that our service or product and the way we are delivering it is meeting their needs, or not.

Sometimes it is their way of telling you that something has changed at their end and they forgot to tell you. Your company may have procedures for dealing with complaints which you should follow.

Half hour with your manager

1. Which people/customers should we particularly focus on and why?

2. What kind of things should I and my team be discussing with customers as and when I meet them?

3. What current opportunities, issues and challenges do we have with our customers?

4. What do I do if I receive a complaint about our work?

5. What lessons have we learnt from customers in the past which have helped us all be more successful?

Notes from the week

Putting feet to your decisions...

This is your first opportunity to take a FROG decision based on your learning this week. Management is about making decisions and then acting on them, so here's your chance.

F **first** thing that you need to do or find out _____
_____
_____

R **resources** - what do you already have in your kit bag to help you
_____
_____

O **others** - any help you need from anyone else to make it happen and why you think this _____
_____
_____

G **go** - a definite step which you will take immediately to put feet to your decision _____
_____
_____

19 Creating personal impact

Now that you have a team and your results are impacting the business in a bigger way then before, you need to think about how you are viewed personally by others. You need to start standing out in a crowd as someone that others wish to do business with, either internally in your company or externally. If people do not know that you and your team exist, it will become harder for you to achieve your results compared with your peers.

Why do you need to make impact?

When you were promoted or recruited to be a manager, the person who made the decision saw something in you that made them believe you could deliver results through a team of people. It is hard, if not impossible, to lead a team invisibly. Maybe you don't like the limelight. Creating impact is not about being the loudest person. It is about ensuring that you allow others to get to know you so that they can start respecting your decisions and ways of working. Over time they will choose which colleagues they will include in their decisions and you may need to be there in order to wield the necessary influence.

Where should I be seen and heard?

This will depend on your job role but some of the places will be

- team meetings
- management meetings
- informal lunches
- corridor conversations
- doing your job at a desk
- with managers who need you or can help you
- with individuals who are struggling
- in congratulating those doing an exceptional job
- with customers
- coaching new colleagues.

What do others need to see and hear?

This will differ depending on your job role. Every individual will have their own opinion as to how they expect you to behave. It is important that you develop your own management persona rather than trying to please everybody all the time.

People read us in three ways

- the words we use or do not use
- the way we speak or whether we are silent
- our body language.

The less we say the more will be remembered. Repeat key instructions. Perhaps you are used to using rough language which some may find offensive. Think about the words you choose – what do they mean? What do they say about you?

Your tone of voice will indicate whether or not you are calm, cross, excited, happy, stressed. Use your voice to add interest to any message. We have been give two ears and one mouth and it is said that that is the ratio in which we should use them.

We can use our body language to walk away from a situation, or to join in. Your face can say a lot. Smile, make eye contact when speaking, Look interested, even if you are tired.

How do I get to know others?

Say hello. This may evolve into a conversation where you can find out what the person's job is and explain what **you** do. You'll discover whether or not it is worthwhile building a better working relationship. In meetings watch for opportunities to share ideas. You have been in management for a few weeks so you should be ready to contribute.

Half hour with your manager

1. What is the impact I have made already?

2. Do I need to change the impression I am making on my team?

3. Do I need to change the impression I am making on you and other managers?

4. Are there internal or customer meetings that I should start attending?

5. What is the easiest way to create a poor impression In this company?

Notes from the week

Putting feet to your decisions...

This is your first opportunity to take a FROG decision based on your learning this week. Management is about making decisions and then acting on them, so here's your chance.

F **first** thing that you need to do or find out _____
_____
_____

R **resources** - what do you already have in your kit bag to help you
_____
_____

O **others** - any help you need from anyone else to make it happen and why you think this _____
_____
_____

G **go** - a definite step which you will take immediately to put feet to your decision _____
_____
_____

20 Team meetings

A team meeting or team briefing is an opportunity to get all your team away from their work. You will be talking with your team in smaller groups and also individually most days as the opportunities arise. To meet with the whole team requires a little more thought and preparation to make the time together worthwhile. Meetings not only require preparation by everyone before hand – they need clear actions afterwards.

Why have a meeting?

It is a good thing to get your team together every now and again. Giving the meeting a focus through a subject or an agenda will help the team pay full attention. Normally meetings are held for

- sales
- to pass on new instructions
- results of quality checks
- updates on company information
- solving a problem

Meetings can be held daily, (sales would be an example of this) weekly, monthly or any other frequency that makes sense in your business.

What do I get from a meeting?

You know that everyone has heard the same information and had the opportunity to question and challenge it. But also you can

- observe the team as they work together
- develop individuals
- demonstrate your management persona
- practice presentation skills
- discover that worries you had about the team are unfounded or confirmed.

What does the team get from a meeting?

It is an opportunity for the team to hear information, share and discuss points together and learn. A well run team meeting can also provide

- a sense of belonging for team members
- an opportunity to contribute
- a forum to voice fears
- some downtime from the daily grind
- chance to work as a team
- personal development
- a chance to volunteer
- fun and relaxation.

How do I plan and run the team meeting?

One thing is absolutely definite – you must plan and think about the meeting before the date because

- everyone will need to rethink their work plans in order to be there
- it is polite to let people know why you are having the meeting and what will be covered so that they can prepare
- meetings must start and end on time – (preparation will help you determine how long the meeting needs to be)
- the team needs time afterwards to action any points that arise
- people's attention span is around 20 minutes, so you need variety during a longer meeting.

Some of the things to prepare would be

- who will chair the meeting
- what goes on the agenda
- any paperwork
- refreshments
- a suitable room.

Half hour with your manager

1. What information will I be getting about the company and from management meetings that should be passed on to my team?

2. How often and how long do you suggest I have team meetings or briefings?

3. How do I book a room for a meeting and where do I get refreshments from?

4. What is the company's view on team away-days?

5. Any hints and tips from your experience of running team meetings to get the best from the time together?

Notes from the week

Putting feet to your decisions...

This is your first opportunity to take a FROG decision based on your learning this week. Management is about making decisions and then acting on them, so here's your chance.

F **first** thing that you need to do or find out _____

_____

_____

R **resources** - what do you already have in your kit bag to help you

_____

_____

O **others** - any help you need from anyone else to make it happen and why you think this _____

_____

_____

G **go** - a definite step which you will take immediately to put feet to your decision _____

_____

_____

21 Getting people to listen

Think for a moment about the people you listen to and why. Perhaps you think of your parents or others who had an influence when you were growing up. Perhaps it was a teacher or university lecturer who had a passion about their subject. Maybe it was a stranger who happened to say something which was very important to you at that moment.

What is listening?

Over the years you will have perfected the art of appearing to listen, but very often actually tuning out, with your mind thinking of other things. We can hear a lot but not remember it. Active listening requires us to give our full attention. There needs to be a 'hook' in what is being said or how it is being said that draws our attention.

As a manager you need to get people to listen to you at certain times – you need to become clever at finding the hooks which make others listen properly. We call it the WIIFM factor – **W**hat's **I**n **I**t **F**or **M**e.

How do I get people to listen?

You do it mainly by developing good relationships and regularly sharing ideas with one another. We build these relationships by

- Speaking with other people so they know we exist
- Taking time to understand what each other does
- Accepting each other for what and who we are
- Respect comes from working together over time
- Trust is what will result.

You also need to become an interesting person, someone that others will want to listen to. This will mean that you are likely to have something relevant and worth saying, and therefore be worth listening to.

What would stop a person listening?

Sometimes it is easier to learn a skill by looking at what not to do. The easiest ways to stop someone listening are

- talking down to them
- not listening to them
- ignoring their ideas
- stealing others' ideas
- giving unasked for advice
- talking for too long
- talking when they have more important things to be doing or thinking about
- being irrelevant
- speaking quietly or cautiously.

So how do I get people to listen?

Get to know people as a normal part of your work. This includes your team, your line manager, other managers and customers. Find out what they are interested in, what their problems are, how you could be useful to them. Be prepared to tell them why you find them worth listening to. What you can do is

- when you do speak, speak clearly
- maintain eye contact with your audience
- ask for their thoughts on what you are saying
- tell them the benefits of your proposal, or outline the problem in terms that matter to them
- invite them to contribute to the discussion
- choose the time and place to when their attention is most likely
- give way if something more important comes up. You can make an opportunity to come back later
- look interested in what you are talking about
- enthusiasm is contagious, but lack of enthusiasm is even more so – this is very important.

Half hour with your manager

1. On a scale of 1 – 10 where 10 means I hold others' attention really easily and 1 means no-one listens to me, where am I?

2. What do **you** need to listen to me for?

3. What is interesting about me and/or what I do that would make others want to listen?

4. How do people get ignored in this company?

5. I am finding it difficult to make headway with certain people in my team or other managers. Any advice on what I need to do differently?

Notes from the week

Putting feet to your decisions...

This is your first opportunity to take a FROG decision based on your learning this week. Management is about making decisions and then acting on them, so here's your chance.

F   **first** thing that you need to do or find out _____

_____

_____

R   **resources** - what do you already have in your kit bag to help you

_____

_____

O   **others** - any help you need from anyone else to make it happen and why you think this _____

_____

_____

G   **go** - a definite step which you will take immediately to put feet to your decision _____

_____

_____

22 Managing conflict

There is no such thing as a difficult person, just a difficult situation. Very occasionally you may be particularly difficult, but the majority of the time it is a situation that leads to conflict. Conflict means that two or more people have opposing views about something. This is a normal everyday occurrence. Sometimes we choose to ignore our conflicting views, sometimes they come out into the open.

Why conflict?

There can be any number of reasons which can trigger conflict. Some are

- going through stressful personal change
- different facts held by different people
- cultural differences leading to clashes in values
- lack of respect has been shown for someone
- change in job or work procedures.

It is very important in a conflict situation to uncover the correct trigger. If you think of someone having an allergic reaction, the first thing you do is discover and remove the trigger for the reaction.

In conflict, be very aware that if it is you that is the trigger, you must remove yourself. If you do not, the conflict is guaranteed to escalate.

What does conflict look like?

You may think that conflict is a sparring match with cross words being spoken, aggressive body language, maybe even tears.

In fact conflict starts inside us, silently. Material ignites and burns gently until something makes it catch fire. Conflict can be an abnormal silence, uncomfortable body language, distraction, irritation. You need to know others well to see the first signs.

How should I, as the manager, deal with it?

If there is a lot of emotion involved, it is best to recognise there is an issue, **defuse any immediate cause of the conflict and take a few minutes to calm down.** A box of tissues in your drawer is a management necessity. At all times, preserve the dignity of all parties. After particularly emotional conflict we can be quite embarrassed to have lost control.

When the time is right, first of all ask open questions to **understand the cause**. Show real empathy and understanding even if you do not initially agree with this. At this stage you are trying to get clear on the issues.

Secondly **share your point of view** and why you think this way. Be assertive – this means that you recognise other peoples' needs but know that your needs are equally important. Just because there is conflict does not mean that you dilute your plans.

Thirdly, try and **mentally distance yourself** from the situation so that you can see both points of view. Maybe take a few minutes break to do this.

To solve conflict see if you can work together to **put options on the table.** Never drive someone into a corner by dictating your solution – this is the easiest way to get a resignation. You may have to say 'no' to something, but the reasons for it must be understood.

What if this doesn't work?

We are only human and your approach may not work, or it may be beyond your experience to deal with. In the first instance refer to your line manager. If you have a Personnel or HR department, someone there may be able to help you.

Half hour with your manager

1. Discuss my natural reaction to conflict situations – avoidance, compromise, dictatorial attitude.

2. What situations have arisen in the past with my team that have lead to conflict?

3. From your experience, what is the hardest thing about managing conflict?

4. If I am in conflict with the way we work together or work you give me to do, how should I let you know?

5. What creates conflict for you - so I can choose to avoid it unnecessarily?

Notes from the week

Putting feet to your decisions...

This is your first opportunity to take a FROG decision based on your learning this week. Management is about making decisions and then acting on them, so here's your chance.

F   **first** thing that you need to do or find out _____

_____

_____

R   **resources** - what do you already have in your kit bag to help you

_____

_____

O   **others** - any help you need from anyone else to make it happen and why you think this _____

_____

_____

G   **go** - a definite step which you will take immediately to put feet to your decision _____

_____

_____

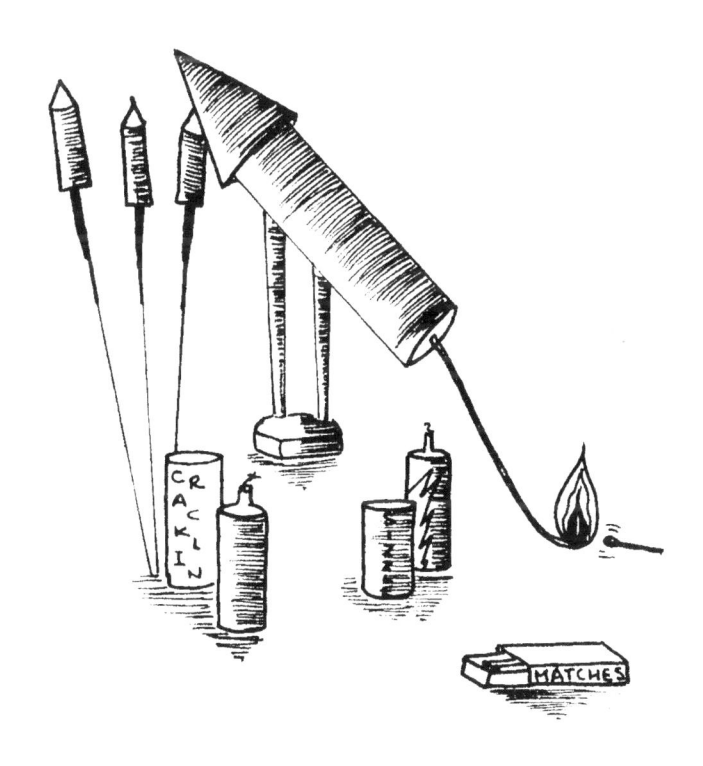

23 Motivating and understanding people

People do things for their own reasons. As a manager I need to inspire my team to be motivated to do their work, and to do it to the best of their ability. Motivated people have more energy and focus. But it is not always so easy to discover what motivates yourself, leave alone each person in your team.

What is motivation?

Motivation is the fuel which drives us and gives us energy. At different times in our lives we are motivated by different things. It could be

- having food and clothing
- having somewhere to live
- feeling I belong and matter to someone
- feeling good about what I have achieved
- reaching out to a new horizon.

Someone who is struggling to pay their mortgage and food bills could be interested in additional duties or overtime if it eased their money worries. A young recruit from college might need clear responsibility and then praise for what they are doing. An experienced colleague may feel a bit bored and need the stimulation of a new challenge.

How do I get to know my team members?

The best way is by making time for them. They are a part of your job role, not an inconvenience. You can diarise certain conversations, like performance reviews and appraisals, but also get used to observing them in the workplace, how they react in meetings and who they keep company with.

Make time for lunch with them. Ask them questions about their interests outside of work and their families. Be prepared to share some of this information about yourself in return.

How do I make work motivational?

If about 65% of our life meets our motivational needs, we can put up with the other 35%. The best advice when you are inexperienced as a manager is to ensure you build balance into the range of work you give your team to do. Vary an individual's work pattern by

- giving them a mix of individual and team work
- encouraging contribution via team meetings and 1:1s
- agreeing performance objectives which make them want to come to work
- broadening their range of work through delegation of your responsibilities
- not allowing them to become a specialist with no under-study.

What does de-motivation do?

Think of a deflated balloon. It looks limp, it may have made a lot of noise as the air went out or it may have silently gone floppy. This is a little like a de-motivated person at work. You recognise them by

- their moaning rather than doing something about a problem
- careless mistakes arising from boredom
- lack of attention when listening – minds are somewhere else which is more interesting
- dependency and comfort in repetitive work
- signs of stress which could mean absence from work.

It is important that you respond to these signs early and reverse any decline before it becomes contagious in your team. Before you do, just make sure that you are fully motivated. The way you feel quickly passes on to the team as well.

Half hour with your manager

1. Discuss what motivates and de-motivates you about your management work.

2. What motivational points are you concerned about in your team?

3. Does my management approach tend to motivate or de-motivate my team? Ask for specific feedback.

4. From your knowledge of my team, how can I organise the work differently to raise the energy levels in any individual?

5. Do you think I have the right level of working relationship with my team, or too much or too little?

Notes from the week

Putting feet to your decisions...

This is your first opportunity to take a FROG decision based on your learning this week. Management is about making decisions and then acting on them, so here's your chance.

F **first** thing that you need to do or find out _____

_____

_____

R **resources** - what do you already have in your kit bag to help you

_____

_____

O **others** - any help you need from anyone else to make it happen and why you think this _____

_____

_____

G **go** - a definite step which you will take immediately to put feet to your decision _____

_____

_____

24 Developing colleagues

A very rewarding part of your management role is to develop the knowledge and skills of your team. You are expected to deliver results consistently. During a year the make up of your team will change. Maybe there is sickness, maternity leave, secondments, promotions or resignations. You cannot guarantee that one person will be replaced by another of equal ability. You need to build as much flexibility into your team as possible.

What is development?

Development means growth. What we need to learn falls into three categories:

- knowledge   - often technical or procedural
- skills   - how we apply knowledge
- behaviour   - how we operate as a workforce.

We work on autopilot much of the time. Once we are familiar with our work, we can generally do it without thinking too much. When challenges and new issues come along they require us to rethink the way we work. We may ask someone's advice. We may need to learn a new set of skills. In this way the workplace allows us to continually learn, and as manager you are the one to oversee and make it happen.

How do I provide development?

You have responsibility for the development of your team, but you do not have to deliver it all. There are a number of ways your team can learn

- induction
- ongoing feedback
- mentoring
- one to one
- training courses
- reading manuals
- on the job
- sharing experiences
- joint projects
- delegation
- chairing meetings.

How do I decide what people need to learn?

As a manager you are given people to work with. They are able to deliver a certain quantity and quality of work. You need to extend their capability to

- keep pace with changes in the workplace,
- help them fulfil their potential
- help them get job satisfaction.

Points to consider are

- build on the skills that new people bring to the job
- have at least two people who know how to do each job to reduce the risk if one is absent
- more experienced people to focus on their work behaviours to help them deliver more with their time, relationships and resources.

What do I need to do?

Performance management reviews are a good time to discuss a person's potential and any development plan. Find out what they want to achieve, any new responsibilities they are looking for. Explain to them the challenges and opportunities facing your team and the business and see what they are interested in.

Talk with the training manager to find out what training and development is available. When someone returns from a training course, find out what they learned and provide them with opportunities to practice new skills and behaviours.

Your team have been learning something from you ever since you became their manager. The way you choose to deal with people, to respond to problems, and to manage your time will all have sent messages to the team that this is how you want them to behave.

Half hour with your manager

1. What do you think my team is learning, or could learn, from me?

2. Who holds the training budget and determines what training courses run?

3. What records do I need to keep of training and development done by the team?

4. What do I need to do to identify developmental needs for the coming 6 months?

5. Are there behavioural competencies in the company?

Notes from the week

Putting feet to your decisions...

This is your first opportunity to take a FROG decision based on your learning this week. Management is about making decisions and then acting on them, so here's your chance.

F   **first** thing that you need to do or find out _____

_____

_____

R   **resources** - what do you already have in your kit bag to help you

_____

_____

O   **others** - any help you need from anyone else to make it happen and why you think this _____

_____

_____

G   **go** - a definite step which you will take immediately to put feet to your decision _____

_____

_____

25 Using technology

Can you imagine an office with rows of filing cabinets, a messenger collecting clerical work delivering it to its next port of call, typists deciphering your handwriting and converting it into reports, documents not received until a day of sending so no replies for a minimum of two days? This was the world in which we managed not so long ago, before technology changed our lives.

How does technology help a manager?

Being able to use technology is now a requirement for most managers – technology which is updated year on year. Managers have no choice but to keep abreast of developments and changes.

Benefits that technology brings to a manager are

- speedy storage and retrieval of up to date information from anywhere we happen to be
- the ability to communicate quickly and directly with anyone whose email address you have
- the creation of documents which look professional and to which you can add over time.

How might I need to use it?

Most companies require managers to use technology for a number of reasons, some of which are

- writing reports
- managing budgets
- presenting information to a group
- sending and receiving emails
- using an online calendar and to-do list
- accessing information from outside the office, either on a laptop or other portable device
- researching information

- training on-line
- video conferencing.

What are the downsides of technology?

For all the benefits of technology in the workplace its use by you and others must be managed carefully.

Data Protection Legislation The law states that no personal data is to be kept on computers unnecessarily. There are strict time limits for storing information. Your company has policies in place to make sure you keep within in the law – check this out.

Loss or theft It is very easy to store information on disks and portable equipment, so the possibility of losing it or having information stolen is high. Company information is confidential and must not fall into the hands of anyone outside. This is important if you work from home or are out on the road.

Do not let technology rule your time On-line communication allows for much quicker responses. There is a tendency to expect replies immediately or to respond to emails as soon as one arrives. Prioritise. Be careful not to pass information on unless the recipient will do something with it.

Downtime The servers which power the network can crash or may need to be reprogrammed. The more dependent a company is on technology the more impact downtime has. If you have a team which works on the network all the time, you will need to plan work for them during any downtime.

Who can help me?

The reality is that most managers teach themselves and learn from one another. You will probably have an IT helpdesk with one or many people available 24/7 to assist you.

Half hour with your manager

1. Who manages the IT helpdesk?

2. What applications should I be using regularly and why?

3. What equipment is available to me and my team – computers, phones and so on. If I want to ask for something new, what is the process?

4. How does our company make sure we meet the requirements of the Data Protection Act?

5. Do I teach myself or are there IT courses I can go on?

Notes from the week

Putting feet to your decisions...

This is your first opportunity to take a FROG decision based on your learning this week. Management is about making decisions and then acting on them, so here's your chance.

F   **first** thing that you need to do or find out _____

_____

_____

R   **resources** - what do you already have in your kit bag to help you

_____

_____

O   **others** - any help you need from anyone else to make it happen and why you think this _____

_____

_____

G   **go** - a definite step which you will take immediately to put feet to your decision _____

_____

_____

26 How am I doing?

If you have worked through a chapter a week, you have now survived at least 6 months in your management role – well done! But how well are you doing and what happens next? It is important for managers to learn about themselves and the impact that they have on those around them. If you start this now, you will find it comes to you naturally as you build up your experience and level of responsibility.

How do I continue to learn?

Hopefully your manager or mentor has found time to work through these chapters with you. If they have, it is unlikely they can continue to dedicate this amount of time to you. It is more likely that you will move to a monthly meeting, and then later quarterly or even half yearly. So you need to start learning for yourself.

Experience is a great teacher. However many management courses you may attend during your career, they will give you guidance but will never cover all the different scenarios you meet in real life.

If you have become used to giving yourself half an hour a week to **reflect** on the week's happenings and the decisions you have made, try to make this a regular feature in your diary. Many managers lose the benefit of experience because they do not stop to realise what they are achieving, to congratulate themselves on what has gone really well, and to think of alternative ways of dealing with situations.

Take time to **learn** new skills and acquire more knowledge by reading, attending meetings, talking with colleagues, coming up with innovative ways of dealing with problems.

Then **test** out your knowledge as soon as possible. This will continue to build your **experience**.

Score yourself

To help you review how well you are doing, here are nine skills you have used in your management work.

C	common sense
O	originality
M	management
P	people
E	ethics
T	tools
E	empowerment
N	nosiness (inquisitiveness)
T	tenacity

For each one read the definition, think back on when you needed to use the skill and score yourself.

- 1 means you haven't used the skill
- 2 means you have used it a little
- 3 means you have used it a lot

Common sense **Score .....**
Use of intelligence, experience and straightforward talking to solve problems, to plan and deal with situations.

Scenarios ....
....
....

Originality **Score .....**
Thinking on your feet, contributing ideas to colleagues and in meetings, not being afraid to take a risk

Scenarios ....
....
....

Management   **Score** .....

Planning work, budgeting, guiding, leading, setting goals and objectives, showing the way, setting a good example, Health and Safety issues, employment law

Scenarios ....

....

....

People   **Score** .....

Developing skills, managing performance, motivating, communicating, disciplining, team meetings, recruiting

Scenarios ....

....

....

Ethics   **Score** .....

Upholding values of the company, learning what you stand for as a manager, stamping your management personality on the team and on your work

Scenarios ....

....

....

Tools   **Score** .....

Use of technology, management information and guidance from your manager, this book and your colleagues

Scenarios ....

....

....

Empowerment   **Score** .....

Getting results through your team, sharing out the work, monitoring performance, taking action when it seems results are not being delivered

Scenarios ....

....

....

Nosiness   **Score** .....

Inquisitive, uncovering potential problems before they become an issue, asking probing questions, using management information to identify issues

Scenarios ....

....

....

Tenacity   **Score** .....

Not giving up, overcoming problems, going the extra distance to achieve results, commitment to company priorities, self-control in emotional situations

Scenarios ....

....

....

How have I scored?   **Total score** .....

Be fair to yourself when you give the ratings – this is only the beginning of your management career so don't expect to have everything right or to have exhausted all the different management challenges. If you can, ask your manager or mentor to rate you as well. See how this agrees or differs from your view.

                                My manager's total score for me .....

What do I do now to become better at managing?

Scored between 9 and 13

Have you been fair to yourself? If you and your manager believe this to be the case, check that your job really is a management role. Ask for more responsibility for people, resources or money. Then perhaps work through the book again. Alternatively you may have found that a management role is not the best use of your skills at this point in your career.

Scored between 14 and 22

You have made a good start to your management career. You have probably faced some challenges already. You have taken some risks and achieved results. For each of the next 6 months you could focus on a particular management skill. On the next page are some suggestions. Agree these with your manager. Start speaking with your training manager to see what management training is available to you and when.

Scored between 23 and 27

It seems that you have a great management role and you are standing up to the rigours of it. If there are any particular parts of the book or competencies where you scored 1 or 2, check with your manager or mentor how you could demonstrate them more. For each of the next 6 months you could focus on a particular management skill. On the next page are some suggestions. Agree these with your manager. Start speaking with your training manager to see what management training is available to you and when.

Suggested management projects for the next 6 months

1. What is the major issue that your manager has with the performance of your team? Plan to remove the issue and deliver required results. Present your plans and then the results formally, in writing and in person.

2. Who is not working to the standard that you believe they could achieve? Take time to sit down with them and understand what they need from you and the company in order to get more job satisfaction. Alter at least one thing to help them change their attitude.

3. What is your personal impact on the team? Be tough on yourself and consider how you are helping or hindering the behaviours of your team. Ask the team how they see you and what they would like you to change in order for them to work better. (This may be a difficult one, but better to find out now than later.)

4. How could you increase productivity, quality or customer service? Work with the team to find ideas and maybe implement something completely new.

5. Watch, listen and feel for how your team and company. operates normally. Ask questions about how things work; why people are doing things a certain way; what their experience is in the company. Is there anything that makes you feel uneasy? Ask questions about it.

6. Find a training programme to support your management career. This could be a management certificate or diploma at your local college giving you a qualification. Alternatively your company may run a management development programme or other short courses which you could attend. Being able to show management training on your CV is always helpful.

About the Author

An inspirational business mentor and interim manager, Beryl Cuckney gets businesses onto a new management footing. Her informed, no-nonsense and confident approach has enabled businesses to restructure in record time without leaving anyone behind. Her advice is based on a wealth of business and management experience coupled with an innate ability to teach.

Until starting her own business - coaching executives in business and mentoring Owner Manager businesses - Beryl has always combined her gift for training and development with hands-on management responsibilities. This has meant she has management experience from supervisory to Managing Director levels in both the public and private sectors. She has designed many innovative management development programmes and trained thousands of managers in manufacturing, telecoms, space, construction, banking, automotive and publishing sectors in the UK, Europe and US, as well as many public sector organisations.

This book consolidates Beryl's experiences and what she has observed in others, and brings it to a wider audience; an audience of first line managers that is often left out of training. The book is also available for companies to personalise or stream on-line via a learning management system (www.yourturn.me.uk).

Printed in Great Britain
by Amazon